AF449689

GINO LEINEWEBER

EVERYTHING IS TRUE

POEMS 2019 – 2022

VERLAG EXPEDITIONEN

Gino Leineweber
Everything is true
Poems 2019–2022

Editor Barry Stevenson, UK
Cover picture Uwe Friesel, Germany
Cover design Birgitta Sjöblom, Sweden
Printed in Germany
ISBN 978-3-947911-75-2

Man can do what he wants
but he cannot want
what he wants
Arthur Schopenhauer
German Philosopher (1788–1860)

GINO LEINEWEBER

EVERYTHING IS TRUE

POEMS 2019 – 2022

Table of Contents

CROCODILE

I am not a crocodile
I am a human being
But I am not a human being
Because I am not a crocodile
Just like a crocodile
Is not a crocodile
Because it is not human
Though it is certain
If it were a man
It couldn't be a crocodile

To some extent, as we can see
our world is quite complex.

In another, though – the void
things are more straightforward.

There I am either not a crocodile
But neither is the crocodile.

CICADAS[1]

The first warm days in May.
Millions and millions of cicadas
emerge from out of the soil
where they have lived for 17 years.
Now it's time for them to climb
    the trees.

When they are high enough to find
    a suitable branch
the females make themselves
comfortable to enjoy the
    spectacular view
while the males are still clinging
    to the tree trunk
trying desperately to catch
    their breath.

Like this one male cicada
that has stopped
for this female
that was sitting above him
    on a branch
and was looking around.

[1] Every 17 years, Brood X cicada emerge from the ground. The insects then shed their exoskeletons on trees. They are endemic in areas throughout the eastern United States, mainly in Virginia and Washington, DC.

14

He, instead of relaxing
after the exhausting climb,
starts singing his brains out.
Just to impress her
for a date with debauchery.

The female, after a while,
got a little bored
Thought:
what the fuck ... let's do it
give the singer his prize.

Alas, he was supposed to die
after he'd got what he wanted,
She can't be blamed,
although little did she know it.
It's just a boy thing

LEAF DESTROYER

I am under the impression
We, the human beings, are
The most intelligent beings
In the world
But I do no longer claim
We are the only ones
With intelligence at all
And I'm not only thinking
Of dolphins, crows, or rats
Nor about my neighbor's dog

Who claims that he, the dog,
Is the most intelligent animal
He has ever happened to meet
Which he proves with
When he goes to his kitchen, or bathroom,
Or elsewhere in his house,
The dog doesn't lift a leg
Or even blink
But when he, the neighbor,
intends to go out
The dog runs to the door
Even when he, the neighbor, hasn't
Lifted his body entirely
From the sofa he, the dog,
is already running to the door.

But I do not mean this dog
I mean a small worm
That lays its eggs
In a leaf
Even though
It has no fingers
To fold it
Instead, it tries hard
To prepare the leaf
So that it can use it
It cuts five leaves from a branch
Then with a small thread
That it spins onto the loose leaves
glues them back onto it
A worm can do such things
Of course, the leaves dry out and curl up.
This is what the worm expected.
It lays its egg
In one of the prepared worm flats
Only in one because of the birds
Birds are curious and wonder
What might be in the rotten leaves
Landing on the branch
They check it and when it's empty
do not bother about the other four
think "shit!" to themselves –

        and fly away

February

February is always underestimated
Not like November
Which makes quite a somber impression
Let alone December
With all that cheery Christmas stuff

January nobody really likes
Instead what a relief when it's finally over
It is always extended by February
Not by a week or a fortnight – no
A bunch of four weeks overtime

However, February is
The most decent month
Its light gives hope to the earth
And while the shadows are shorter
Every day is getting longer

Without February what else
Could hide springtime
Or other secret stuff
That might trigger hot anticipation
For a wonderful year ahead

For us to appreciate the treasure
Try taking a glance behind the curtain
Instead, we walk only looking down
Griping shaking whining
Cold – snowy – wet

GRASS CONCERT

You know the idiom
Listening to the grass grow

I asked myself
How ridiculous is that?

I can't hear the grass grow.
I am also sure that no one can
Until I read an astonishing opinion
That says some animals could

Okay – the question is
How do they know?

Did these animals tell them?
If so – Which ones?

A zombie is a small yellow flower
After a line from the Greek movie *Dogtooth*

It is actually not true
But what's a zombie anyway?

Don't come to me with:
    Look at the encyclopedia

It is full of fake news
Or alternative facts

I figure such things out
Rather by me myself

My first idea
Due to the word's diction
It's some kind of a being

It is neither a flower
Nor an animal
Although it could be one:

Imagine a drunken hyena

Rosy Rhodian pebbles by the Aegean Sea
    look for attention
when I am going for my morning swim
and even as I adore these dear pebbles
it looks like they won't let me go into the
    water easily

When a tired evening sun wraps the sky
    and the clouds
with colors I haven't even known before
    they exist
the taverns turn on their lights and fulfill
    the island's lot
by providing a vivid night with talk with
    tasty local wine and food

With different influences from abroad from
    the earliest times until now
the island's rugged landscape covered with
    lovely pine and cypress
with vineyards and remarkable olive trees
    vindicates the promise
the special impression that gave me the
    feeling of 'love at first sight'

Having coffee in the afternoon in front
    of walls
that are hiding behind curls of lilac
    bougainvillea
I understand my inner mental condition
    and the way the island
always translates it by conjuring a
    magic smile on my face

Funeral

Make sure I will be buried
On a day like this

When the sun
Needs time
To arrive

Weary almost
From arising

But eager
To dry
The tears of the night

Ardent to embrace
The happy day

Kisses
With glossy lips
The colored leaves

Those
The wind will cause
The genes to fly

Make sure I will be buried
On a day like this

SHE

Her
world alone enchants her.
She doesn't notice anything around her.
Just enjoys herself.

But I am directly under her spell.

Suddenly
She takes a grape and looks at me
With eyes like two flowers in eternal
    serenity.

For a while I can't breathe.

Her look causes no reflection on her part
She isn't even aware of where she is
    at this moment
let alone a little consideration as to
    who the hell
it might be that surrounds her:
Me

Who has lost himself in her forever.

He can't stand her anymore. Thirty years
    and a bit.

He doesn't blame her that his wrinkles
    make his face look sour,
while hers
make her look funny and sympathetic.

He blames her for her cheerfulness,
which he knows perfectly well
is deceptive – it is not in her character
    at all.

He knows she's just pretending.
Only for the single desire
to make him suffer!

Colette

Colette lives in Paris
Struggles for what has been stolen
By her first husband
The name on the books she wrote
She kisses Missy
Gives the world a stage for truth
Has to live as a vagabond

Colette loves Missy
Lives with beggars and drunkards
Is friends with journalists and writers
The lover of De Jouvenel –
First the father then later the son
She overtrumps society
With the questioning eye of a wise woman

Colette writes novels
Becomes famous with
Chérie and *Awakening Hearts*
Composing in it love troubles in purple
And narratives in taboo
In defiance of her time
A woman that is who she thinks she is

I HAVE DONE NOTHING

From one day to the next
I lost a close friend
With whom I also
Was in business

I didn't know why
Years and years later
I got to know
But only from a third party

This friend used to have
A beautiful girlfriend
Which isn't bad on one hand
Unless you are the jealous type

Arguments all night long
Once she finally cried:
    Yes! I fucked him and when I can
    will do it again and again

However, that was not true
But my friend had this obscure fame
He couldn't suffer for innocence anyway
… Aren't we all sinners by birth?
    —

Enfold
  pinch
    handle
      overspend

She had called herself an artist,
worked with bodies as a canvas.

That love-making-art could take weeks,
months, years, or just a little hour.

When her creation was complete,
after capturing every speck,
every morsel of a figure,
when there was nothing left to do,
she would look for another canvas
another male or female body

To a specific extent, though,
it was a hidden art because
the people around didn't notice.

Maybe you can't call it art then,
  can you?
    Anyway,
      she quit.

I LOVE YOU AS YOU ARE

I love the way
You care for me
I love the way
You smile at me

I love it
When you wake me up
Even without thinking
And when we're making love
Breathing moaning sighing

However,
What I really hate is
That I don't have any clue
Who, for heaven's sake, are you?

He was telling me
I'm not the girl
he thought I was

I was the girl
of what I thought to be
I was neither

And he the guy
that is what he thought
he wasn't either

I cut him off
and was the girl
I always knew I was

It's Better

She doesn't know
Anything
Under the moon

He walks home
The rest
is sleep

SLEEP

Listen to the evening wind's music
looking forward to
the night's kisses from her cryptic mouth
that holds you with her hidden hand

On the way to bed
you are like a child
who bravely awaits it
as a tangible comfort

You are used to
sounds in the midnight gaze
which ease the pain
and mend your broken heart

Caresses of sleep
play with your unwillingness
and provide you
a serene awakening

Debauchery

She ordered spaghetti as everyone else
Nothing special to mention in that
But she is pretty and vivacious.

Sometimes she bowed her head
Onto the plate, downs the noodles
Like a predator
Or held her fork in the air
Twirled the Spaghetti around
Chews the morsel she has created
Then looking suspicious
As if on the plate
She could have missed something.
Besides, in a vibrant way
She talks to her friends
Pivoting her empty left hand
Revealing her points.

Did I mention she has these teeth
I like it so much in girls?
It's called an overbite.

I always expect
One of these
One day
One catch
Will devour me

Jesus H. Christ

I do not believe in evolution.
Starting as an assumable happy unit
finally doing the uncomfortable separation
without a hint of blame.

It does not seem plausible at all.
As well as the bold claim
everyone of our predecessors
was swimming in the sea

If that is true the question is
why 'on earth' or 'the hell'
do we all save money over a year
to spend our holidays on beaches?

Furthermore, when we should have evolved
from monkeys and gorillas
why in 'Jesus H. Christ's' name
do we still act like them?

Lost Innocence

The loss of innocence
Does not mean
Becoming guilty

Innocence is nothing other
Than not knowing
– Like a state of mind

When this condition is lost
It can never be replaced.

Some physical states
Are thought of in the same way.

Such as virginity
Which is not lost
In a rightful way
And therefore leads to shame
In a religious sense

It points, rightful or otherwise,
To a material condition.

The good news is
There is no innocence at all.

Just as there is no guilt

In a criminal sense (one might call it so)
– There is only a kind of responsibility

When knowledge is called guilt
The necessary counterpart
Is innocence

– Hence, nothing other than ignorance.
Since it is the counterpart to knowledge

The loss of innocence
Means nothing other than
One is no longer an idiot

Stag Metamorphosis

Homage to Ovid

The best-unarmed protection
against a familiar aggressor
is yelling defensively:
  It's me, it's me – Don't shoot

Or raising your arms protectively
In front of you
Hands with the palms
Toward the aggressor

Or both

Alas, If you're a stag
Neither of these
Is an option

Temperature

Hot like
Hell and wrath

Warm like
Luck and happiness

Cool like
Love and compassion

Calm like
Heaven and equanimity

The Lone Wolf

It was always me
The lone wolf that I am

I did my whole life
What I wanted to do

Some things turned out badly, some silly.
However, most turned out
The way that pleased me
And success – of course
Kind of – it happened sometimes
I do not know what my life
Would have been without it
Most likely depressed

Or not – you don't miss what you don't know

Anyway, it was always me
If that may change – say I wouldn't any longer
Be able to live my life that way –
I might have
To depend on other people
Then I would know for sure
I would no longer want to live
The only way to call it my life
Is to live it the way I want to

However,
There is no my life
There is no I and no me either
Only the delusion of a self
That's what I was talking about

My grip on the I-concept of the mind
Is an entity … the body I watch
But when I haven't done all that I wanted to
Then, who was it?
And what is it I am doing right now?

I don't know

Like imagining the beginning
The unimaginable energy of movement
Call it, whatever you like
Namely the force that was necessary.

Life was always in my mind
The will to live – to move
Means that the I-concept demands action
It made me a person to be recognized for
My deeds, my education, my love,
My aversions, my temper – you name it

But I was determined to follow the will
And I did so
And I will be doing so, whether I want it or not.

Movement

Movement is life
Life is movement

When you were born
As a runner
Then you have to run

If as a walker
You have to walk

Born as a sitter
You must sit
No movement

Shit

Time doesn't care
But it isn't easy to come by
Since we're so used to it

Time doesn't care
What we do
Or where we live
Whom we love
Or fight off

It doesn't even care
If we are alive

Why the heck
Are we then
So occupied with it?

FIRST NATION

The first people
spontaneous beings
created by divine breath
made up of flesh and blood and a spirit
instead of rock, or fire, or water, or wind
the first nation, the Anishinabek

All flora and fauna surrounding them
as much a part of nature as they are
watched by eagles
not just birds
but the celestial messengers
between the Creator and the Anishinabek

Prophecies pointed to European invaders
they came, the eagles left, the first nation
    was destroyed
but the last and seventh prophecy says
it will rise again:
when the bald eagles return
so also, the Anishinabek

What If

People are pretty strange people.
Not everybody; nonetheless,
I could point out many things about most
But above all, they like to annoy

Yet it affects them in both cases
At first, it mightn't be enough to annoy
    others
Secondly, they don't see the effect on
    themselves
Don't even realize it either

Why do they do it at all?
It cannot be just out of ego
Since some do it anonymously

Anna, who is looking over my shoulder
at the question on the paper,
Eerily for me as always,
says:
    It's escapism

I wonder at first how she
Knows the word at all.

And secondly, what if
She is right?

Aristotle Buddha Muhammad Jesus
    Lao Tse et al
the great masters of the world were
    creators
they did not tell the truth
they didn't even intend to either.
The truth, one can't explain with
    words.

Hence their speeches were
stories and poetry
which were full of metaphors.
Although they have penetrated our
    minds
the masters spoke to our spirit.

People that are under the impression
they have heard the truth about
    reality
are unintentionally misled by the
    texts
since they aren't anything but art,
which isn't always realistic.

Slaves

We were all born into slavery.
No longer
In the sense
It's mostly understood

However, figure this:
Isn't all that you do
Pressured by third parties?

Education is to prepare you.
Then you work and act
For others

Although they say
You do it for money

But what if
you don't need money?

Planet Earth

In the universe, there
wobbled around an orb
of radiated heat
a planet

Picture it with water, earth and fire.

A blue marble with oceans and continents
with a range of thousands of miles
full of life and fate

Picture it as a lively maze

All you have to do is go through it
because at the end of this whirlwind
is an award

If you can see the planet
Its water and earth and fire
… That's very good

However,
… the planet doesn't exist

You've created it in your mind.

There is no water, no earth, no fire
but the idea of it dominates
your every living moment.
At the end, you will be aware
It was only a segment of the imagination

Anyway,
You had no chance to escape
Since the planet is a labyrinth

Everything that is –
Is without me

Everything that happens –
Comes without me

Everything observed –
Is watched without me

Because there is no me

Limbo

he awoke
had to pee
the bed collapsed

later that night
it happened again
the bed collapsed

dream and reality seem alike
scary without
the collapsing

He awakes again
in reality or not
the bed collapses

TH E Y

ride, ride, ride
to the sun, sun, sun

run, run, run
from the sun, sun, sun

way too hot!

didn't he know it in the first place?
    he did!

did it anyway?
    he did!

why?
    since they told him

they?
    yes, they

SAYING GRACE

My weapon of choice
Is my grace
Do I have a definition
Of grace
Other than thinking
Is it my hairdo?

Everybody is sitting around the table
Drinking wine from crystal glasses
Lighting more candles than necessary
Pestering each other with talk
Laying their ears on the tracks,
Yet hearing nothing

Yes, I know, I reply to myself:
My grace comes from inside
And my power
And everything

However,
I am alone
Who cares?

DISCRIMINATION

Discrimination is not pretty.
But if everybody does it
from time to time at least
there could be a market
for creating a database
to trade with it

We have it with trading emissions.
Which aren't nicer either
I could – let's say – an old N-word
that's been lying around for years
and I do no longer want to use it
put on this database

If there is someone
who really needs to discriminate
he or she might be in dire need
of having my old N-word.
It could then be taken out of my account
and transferred to his or hers

The benefits would be obvious.
I'd get rid of my discriminating word
would no longer have to chasten myself.
The new owner doesn't need to do this either
It isn't his or hers – it's mine
But nobody knows

MIDDLEMAN

Imagine

Two cyclists
Riding from north and south
Toward each other on a path

The northerner is a middleman by birth
He will not give way at all
In his world the other has to

But he is also a middleman
… Boom!

I want
to be beautiful
similar to the sun
to shine every day

I want
to be like the sound
that rises like a whisper
between you and me

I want a higher power
to saves us
for infinity

FOR WHOM THE BELL TOLLS

All I see is nothing
So what?

I don't really know
What I am looking for.

Some day
I might

Anyway, in the spring
I never wait for the autumn

In the summer
Never look for the winter

It might never come
I could have heard the bell tolling

Lockdown Surviving Poem

To Lutz

I was walking
Around the house
And was thinking
Thinking about –
What?

I do not know

In the process
When you think,
You would not think
What you think

Later, when you think
The thing is
You think
What you thought

It's just like this:

Thoughts don't come
And introduce themselves
You have to figure it out
Figure out –
What?

Refugees

An enormous number of people,
who were starving or at the edge of society
were drawn to another world

With big hopes for happiness and bliss
going for the promised land of money and
fortune,
no matter how to get at it

The masses were hard to control.

There were hundreds of thousands
from villages and towns
from all over Europe once
on their way to the New World

FEAR IS NOT EXPECTED

People who are leaving their countries
Either looking to get a better life
Or escaping violence and war
Are not coming as immigrants

They come as refugees
Or as workers to earn money
Least of all for themselves
Mainly for their families back home

They mostly did not choose this
Did not think about the consequences of
Accessing another land and culture
To evade the suffering at home

The impulse to strive for the best
For oneself and especially for children
Is evident in every life
Not only in human beings

Equally present in people's life is fear
Fear of leaving
Fear of a new and unknown situation
Fear of some strange environment

Only if this fear
Is less than the anxiety
Related to the current situation
Are human beings ready to move

Everyone leaving home
Escaping their mother country
Either hopes to find a better life
Or, in despair, wants to escape violence

They meet societies
struck by fear as well
People imagining losing their lives and
traditions
Which they long to preserve

Refugees are not intent on destroying nations or
societies
What they do not expect is fear
What they expect is compassion
What they expect is to be allowed in

FATHER (1)

My father my father
You left for eternity

But you shouldn't have done
As you shouldn't have done either
What you did for the sake of your son

When I left in adolescence
I tried to find myself.

However, what I found
When looking at me
Was you – always you

FATHER (2)

It is the truth.
The death of a father
is the most crucial incident
in the life of a man

It is also the truth
you do not know
until it occurs

The mourning that is now going
to embrace you and hold you
instead of your father
will stay for a lifetime

Lucky you.
Having had someone you loved

Because that feeling
will not die

I am not twenty
I don't have a beautiful body

However,
I am on vacation

Musings about *Everything is true*
by Uwe Friesel

Upon reading the poems of my poetry pal and colleague Gino Leineweber, I must admit I don't really know him. Or – more precisely – I found it rather difficult to enter the poetic world, which unfolds in the volume *Everything Is true.*

My hesitation has to do with Buddhism and the notion of future life. Being absolutely against any form of religion (Leineweber maintains Buddhism is a philosophy) I neither tend to Christian *Eternity* nor to *Nirvana* of Buddhism, Sufism or other -ism. That includes Capitalism and Communism, which are nowadays dealt with like religions by their ardent followers. I prefer humanism.

Therefore, I was stunned to realize the keyword in the whole book is compassion especially to be found in the two poems *Refugees* and *Fear is not expected.* The poem *Refugees,* of course, evokes TV pictures of people trying to escape the darkness and no-future of Africa, Afghanistan, Iran and, alas, Ukraine. But when the text has nearly reached its end, Gino reminds us of the

Europeans, who once fled from their misery in Europe to the New World. *A New World,* mind you: To be created by fugitives and refugees, who had crossed the ocean because of utter hopelessness in the *Old World.*

And then, after that startling reminder, another actual and moving poem follows, entitled *Fear is not expected.* It is true: They appear at our shores naked and poor, those refugees, just like those who once had arrived at the shores of America. But now, it is not money they expect most, says Gino. What they expect is compassion instead of rejection.

Compassion – for what? Christians might say: for God's whole creation. Buddhist Gino says: for all beings on earth. In short: compassion for life.

He wonders: To what end? Who am I myself? What is love? Do we know whom we love? Aren't we just an illusion of ourselves, like the shadow on the wall of Platon's cave? Questions that may fill up a whole life of meditation, I'm sure.

Or take the eternal riddle, "Can men understand women?" At first sight, it seems to be the superficial rhetoric of gender prepotency. But why does one single look into a woman's eye make a man (a poet) shiver lifelong, whereas she eats grapes in all innocence, with him watching her breathlessly all the while?

In the end, it seems that life has neither entrance nor exit. Time leaks out. The blue planet earth is a mere invention of our brain because all is imagined, except for serenity – the absolute calm. Nirvana.

Being an agnostic myself, I try to imagine Nirvana. But I can't. I have no clue, not even a metaphor for the great void. But then, reading Gino Leineweber, at least I get a hint of what he is after.